How to Mitigate PLEAS

By
Dawn Wilkinson

Paperback Edition First Published in Great Britain in 2023 by Dawn Wilkinson

ISBN: 9798396337428

Copyright © Dawn Wilkinson 2023

Dawn Wilkinson has asserted her rights under 'the Copyright Designs and Patents Act 1988' to be identified as the author of this work.

All rights reserved.

No part of this document may be reproduced or transmitted in any form or by any means, electronic, mechanical, photocopying, recording, or otherwise, without prior written permission of the Author.

Other books by Dawn Wilkinson:

An eBay life for me

Diary of an eBay seller

Where is my item?

Acknowledgements

As always, I am thankful and blessed to have my wonderful family and my partner Gary in my life.

Gary, you make me laugh everyday – to be fair it's not always intentional on your behalf, but very entertaining for me.

My mother, **Maureen** who encourages and supports me no matter what. She has been instrumental in my positive attitude to life.

I am truly blessed to have a wonderful network of supportive friends, many of whom I am proud to say are solid truth seekers and critical thinkers!

A very special thanks to **Angela Craddock** who kindly provided the foreword and back cover blurb for this book. Angela you are a very talented author and I know you are going to go far!

A special mention also to **Adrienne** who has always offered advice to the content of my books.

A huge Thank you to **Caz,** a relatively new member of my truth-seeking community who has been a very encouraging influence on me. She often tells me how wonderful I am! It's her fault I am going to attempt an open mic night at a comedy club. She laughs at my jokes, but I have to say *Caz, I don't find you funny at all* – I'm joking!

Foreword

Top rated eBay seller and successful author Dawn expresses her gratefulness to the universe for what she has. Her attitude of gratitude, sense of humour and desire to help others is what makes Dawn shine out from the crowd. Now she wishes to share how she gets the best out of life to enable her readers to achieve positive things for themselves.

We all have busy lives, routines and habits that we fall into. We allow these things to control us. It's always beneficial to take a fresh look at things, to look up at the sun, sniff the air, to literally wake up and smell the coffee. Our mindset can influence how our day evolves, whether it turns out to be a good one or not, but do you think your fate is controlled by others, luck (or lack of it) or the universe? The word *fate* mostly has a negative connotation, indicating that people can do nothing about the future, and everything is the way it is. Now try viewing fate as divine re-alignment. What about YOU? It is you who holds the power, you are in charge of your destiny though you may need to be reawakened, reminded that you are in control and not simply a back-seat-passenger in this life journey. It's all about you!

Throw a pebble in a lake and watch the ripples spread out across the surface of the water. In this same way, we all have the ability to reach out, to influence and affect others. Small acts of kindness can create huge impact on others, including ourselves, as giving makes us feel good and pays us back in unexpected ways. Now, imagine how far those ripples could reach out if we all were more thoughtful, innovative and generous. The world would indeed be a better place. Small ripples can gain the momentum to create waves.

Dawn would like you to re-evaluate your life and press a re-set button. She wants you to do more of the things that make you happy and to manifest and seize opportunities to improve life. Think about what raises your vibe and know that you are the epicentre. Embrace the opportunity to transform karma into your destiny.

No doubt you put the needs of others above your own but now Dawn appeals to you to take time out for yourself and work through her *Pleasure Principle.* Do the exercises to find out what resonates with you. What changes will you make? You will be surprised how great it feels to be the Captain of your Soul. Spread the ripples, spread the word, pay it forward.

By Angela Craddock

Contents

Introduction	11
P is for	15
L is for	24
E is for	33
A is for	42
S is for	51
U is for	59
R is for	67
E is for	73
The Soundtrack	75
Part Two – Exercises	78

Introduction

Poor is the man whose pleasure depends on the permission of another.
Madonna

So, you want to live a life of PLEASURE, well you've bought the right book! You will not be disappointed. This book has some amazing advice and techniques you need to apply to your life to transform your experience in this material world.

As the Madonna quote above implies you are responsible for achieving pleasure and not giving your power to another to give you permission to achieve a pleasurable life.

Each letter of the word PLEASURE will start a new chapter in this book. In each chapter you will find a list of principles to apply to your daily life. If a principle does not resonate with you, don't worry. Move onto the next one and see if that resonates. Ideally, I want you to pick at least one principle out of each chapter and create your list of principles to live by. Of course, you may be smarter than me and think of your principle for that letter, which I haven't covered. The purpose of this book is to make you think about life, your life in fact. What makes you happy? What makes you unhappy? What do you want to manifest? What does your ideal life look like?

Part two of this book includes exercises for you to complete in order to put these principles into practice. Remember, only follow the principles that resonate with you. If they all resonate, then that's awesome.

While I was meditating recently, I wondered about the meaning of life. I have been told by various spiritualists that we choose to come here for this earthly experience. As I write this book in 2023, I am sure I do not have to remind anyone of the world events from 2020 onwards. As I have experienced every emotion going through this period, I pondered to myself why would I agree to come here for this? So, I asked Spirit *why did I agree to come here?* The answer I instantly received was *'Pleasure',* hence the inspiration for this book.

I believe I did not come here for a miserable existence - I came here for pleasure. By applying these principles to my life and importantly changing my perspective I have looked at all the positive things that have happened over the last three years. I've met some wonderful like-minded people. I've tuned into the power of manifestation. If the last three years has taught us anything, it should hopefully be appreciation for life.

We are living through challenging times, but I know we can get through this. We need to unleash the power of manifestation that is within us all. As Madonna says *'I want to start a revolution of love. Are you ready?'*

Yes, I'm ready Madonna! (Have you realised I'm a huge Madonna fan yet?)

Reader, are you ready?

Yes! I hear you shout, well let's get cracking then!

Oh, just one more thing…. (I love *Columbo*!) You may find many of these principles link nicely to each other. Once you put one of these principles into practice you will find another principle can then easily be applied.

On the other note, you will also find that some of these principles seem to contradict another. I make no apology for this – it is entirely deliberate! Life is full of contradictions. When we play the game of life many people play by different rules that's why there is so much conflict! Unfortunately, there is no one size fits all. That's why I urge everyone to play the game of Manifestation!

By following these principles, I am sure you will transform your life and bring so much more pleasure into this magical experience.

P
is for.....

PLEASE YOURSELF

We often use the phrase of 'Please yourself' as an insult: Definition:

Used to express indifference, especially when someone does not cooperate or behave as expected.

However, I think if we want to live a life of pleasure we initially must start within. As the popular hymn suggests:

Let there be peace on earth and let it begin with me.

It's time to really think about your life:

What do you want from life?
What pleases you?
What brings you pleasure?
How many times do we put other people's needs ahead of our own?
Why do we feel selfish if we refuse to do something we simply don't want to do?

To truly live a life of pleasure you need to start being honest with people. It doesn't mean you are a bad person if you decide to put your desires first. Many human beings can be described as 'people pleasers' but not many people are called 'self-pleaser'. Instead, the word 'selfish' is used. To manifest a new reality, we need to re-program our minds. Putting our needs first is not about being selfish it's about self-care and preservation. There are some brilliant videos on YouTube on how to stop being a people pleaser.

People pleasing is no longer an option. Because I'm adopting the radical belief that my ideas, my thoughts as well as my feelings matter too.

Please Yourself can also mean Please take care of yourself.

****

PACK IT IN

This applies to many different aspects of life.
If you have bad habits that are affecting your health – **Pack it in!**
If you are in a relationship with someone who does not appreciate you or treat you with respect – **Pack them in!**
If you are constantly moaning about how bad your life is – **Pack it in!**
If you are spending money you haven't got – **Pack it in!**
I'm sure you get the idea. Anything that lowers your vibration and has a negative impact on your life you need to …..**Pack it in!**
Make changes that improve your life instead of lowering your vibration by constantly complaining. This will only lower your mood causing depression.

A bad habit never disappears miraculously, it's an un-do it yourself project.
Abigail Van Buren

When you decide to break a relationship or friendship with someone it doesn't mean you don't care about them any more. If that person is having a detrimental impact on your life you need to take action to protect yourself. It may mean taking time out from that person and focusing your attention on lifting your vibration before seeing them again.

Never wish harm to anyone. Sometimes a little time apart is good for a relationship:

Absence makes the heart grow fonder.

Making your friends and family aware of boundaries you set is also beneficial. We will cover this later in the book, but as this is important to protect yourself, I thought I would mention it here as well.

****

PLAY OUT

Remember when you were a child and you felt so alive playing out with your friends.

We are young, we run green, Keep our teeth nice and clean
See our friends, see the sights, Feel alright.
Supergrass – Alright

You didn't worry about the time; you didn't worry about tomorrow. Wait …. You didn't worry! Fast forward to adulthood when you worry about the bills, about work, family and friends. Obviously, we are always going to have concerns for family and friends, it's only natural to care.

The principle of Play Out means stop putting off something you want to do because of expectations of others. Be like a child every now and then. That doesn't mean scream on the floor of the supermarket if they haven't got your favourite wine in stock – it doesn't go down too well, and you will get a few weird stares! However, on that note we can learn something from children. They seem to know they need to scream and voice what they want to manifest it. So, whenever you feel the Universe is dealing you an unfair hand in life – Scream and demand a reshuffle!

Anyway, back to playing out.

How many times do we get invited somewhere we really want to go, but we've got household chores to do, or we have committed to do something for someone else? When someone rings you up and asks you to play out re-arrange things to accommodate what you want to do. If you can't re-arrange engagements, then plan a new play date. We need contact and socialising is a vital part of your life of pleasure. We lift each other's spirits in so many ways. So go…. Play out!

The world is your playground.

****

PERSONAL RESPONSIBILITY

We spend so many times making excuses and giving our power away to others. We are personally responsible for our experience on earth.

You must begin to understand that the present state of your bank account, your sales, your health, your social life, your position at work, etc., is nothing more than the physical manifestation of your previous thinking.
Bob Proctor

Of course, things will happen that are out of our control, but we can control how we react. Yes, we all make mistakes and wish we could go back in time and change things. Cher had a hit song about this issue! The truth is we cannot go back in time.

Another important part of improving relationships is by taking responsibility for our actions, which also encourages others to take note.

Enjoy this experience. Yes, you'll make mistakes, but learn from them. Own your mistakes. Take responsibility for your actions.

The choices we make are ultimately our own responsibility.
Eleanor Roosevelt

You have the power to manifest the reality you want. It's time to look at all aspects of your life and find balance. Download a copy of the life wheel from the internet and assess each aspect. What can you improve in your life? What problems can you accept that have been caused by your own actions?

Take responsibility for this experience in the physical world – we've all heard the saying 'Life is what you make it'.

****

PRAISE

How often do we praise ourselves and others? We have a habit of focusing on when someone lets us down or says something hurtful. It's time to change focus to the good deeds.

Give Praise liberally and take it with grace.

Start praising or thanking someone when they do a good deed for you. Don't forget to praise yourself, give yourself a proverbial pat on the back when you succeed at something or help someone out. Even when you control your temper and not allow an argument to develop, give yourself some praise. By acknowledging your own achievements and accomplishments you help build your self-esteem and self-confidence. This will then help motivate you to continue to strive towards more goals and push yourself towards greater success. If you are trying to lose weight for example, congratulate yourself even if it is not as much weight as you would have liked to have lost. Don't reward yourself with a slice of cheesecake (or glass of wine!) – I've tried this in the past, turns out it only cancels out the good work you had done – who knew!

When you praise others for their good deeds and successes this can help strengthen relationships. It helps build trust and rapport, therefore creating a positive and supportive atmosphere. This can then have a ripple effect as the positive vibes spread out to touch other lives. Encouraging others to carry on achieving their goals.

Practising gratitude and expressing appreciation can improve physical and mental health. This means a reduction in stress, anxiety, and depression which can only be beneficial to us in our pursuit of happiness.

Praise is the mode of love which always has some element of joy in it.

C. S. Lewis

PERSPECTIVE

It's all about perspective. Bob Proctor said:

Change your perspective, change your reality.

Share your problems with someone you can confide in. It's amazing how people's perspective about the same situation can differ. It helps us gain new insights and a deeper understanding by changing our viewpoint. This can lead to developing empathy for people and becoming more open-minded in the process.

Changing your perspective can help you overcome challenges and obstacles in life. By looking at a problem from a different angle could help find new solutions or opportunities that you may have previously overlooked. This may help you take control back and develop resilience for future situations.

By opening yourself up to new viewpoints you can also open many new opportunities in life. This can then lead to new experiences, hobbies and more people to play out with!

I used to hate food shopping. I always end up on the slowest moving checkout. There's always a screaming child in my vicinity! I have now chosen to change my perspective to make this chore more tolerable. I now enter the supermarket giving thanks and feeling blessed that there is food on the shelves. I don't mind standing in the slowest queue as I love to listen in on people's conversations! Oh, and that screaming child – Well, I appreciate the fact that it's **NOT** my screaming child!

Some things in life are bad. They can really make you mad.
Other things just make you swear and curse.

When you're chewing on life's gristle. Don't grumble, give a whistle. And this'll help things turn out for the best.
Always look on the bright side of life.
Monty Python
****

PRIORITISE

Many people cannot prioritise. However, it's an essential skill that must be learned. When you master how to prioritise you can eliminate so much stress from your life. The skill of prioritizing is crucial in both personal and professional life. It allows individuals to effectively manage their time and resources and focus their energy on the most important tasks and goals. Prioritising helps people make informed decisions and enables them to identify and address urgent and critical issues before they become unmanageable. Relieve pressure at work by learning how to prioritise. By allocating your time more wisely, it will stop you being so stressed at work and allow you to start enjoying your job. There is no reason why anyone should be miserable in their employment. If you are miserable then you need to address the reasons for this. If you know you are in the wrong job, then you need to act and do something about it.

Life's too short to be spent in a job you hate.

In your personal life the skill of prioritising will mean less stress and anxiety. You need to achieve balance in your life.
Are you rushing around like a headless chicken every morning?

This isn't a good start to the day as you start the day in stressed mode.

Could you get up a few minutes earlier?

Could you go to bed a little earlier the night before? Could you delegate some household responsibilities to lighten your load?

__Make sure your priorities are aligned with your values and your vision.__

L

is for.....

LAUGH

Make sure you find time to laugh every day. I know there are times when people don't feel like laughing but believe me 'laughter is the best medicine'. Laughter releases endorphins in the brain (feel-good chemicals). So, by watching a comedian or a funny film, it can lift our spirits in times of low mood. It is said that the sound of a cat purring can have healing benefits. Laughter is our equivalent of a cat purring. According to www.scientificamerican.com, cats purr during inhalation and exhalation with a consistent pattern and frequency between 25 – 150 hertz.

I know many people who are grieving the loss of a loved one often feel guilty if they experience happiness or laughter, as if it is somehow disrespectful to the person in spirit. If you were to pass into spirit, would you want your loved ones left on the earth plane miserable and in grieving? No, I think not! Never forget your loved ones but remember the happy memories that bring a smile to your face. Laughing makes us more optimistic which can only raise our vibration. Having a laugh with friends or family strengthens our relationships and provides more happy memories. So, bring more joy and positivity into your life, find time to sit back with a cuppa and a good comedy. Plan a night out with friends or a family dinner. Spend time with people you love, have a laugh, and create some fantastic memories together.

Finding the funny in a situation can also help relieve tension in difficult times. Focusing on the positive can also reduce feelings of hopelessness and despair. Therefore, developing stronger resilience.

Research has shown that people with a positive outlook at life experience greater satisfaction – more pleasure! They also have stronger immune systems, lower blood pressure and reduced risk of chronic diseases and depression. So go on, have a laugh!

Why so serious?
Joker (Batman The Dark Knight)
****

LEARN

Learn something new every day. We've all heard the saying:

Every day is a school day.

Learn from past mistakes. Learn from other people's mistakes. Take inspiration from other people. We live in a time when we have so many opportunities to help each other through the power of social media and YouTube. It's amazing how many people want to share knowledge and help other people. I have been inspired by so many wonderful people on YouTube.

Expand your horizons by learning new skills. Achieve greater success and fulfilment in life.

Don't use the excuse *I'm too old* – age is just a number. Don't use the excuse *I can't afford it* – Check out online and you will find many opportunities for learning for free!

Don't use the excuse *I'll never be able to do that* – well, how will you know if you don't try? In the words of David Fishwick *'Do something because it's always better than doing nothing.'*

> ***The more that you read, the more things you will know. The more that you learn, the more places you'll go.***
> Dr. Seuss, (I Can Read With My Eyes Shut!)

Being adaptable to learning new skills can also bring more job opportunities into your life.

> ***Let the improvement of yourself keep you so busy that you have no time to criticize others.***
> Roy T. Bennett, (The Light in the Heart)

Opening ourselves up to new skills can also lead us to join classes or groups which is great for mental health. Connecting with new people which can then create more opportunities to come your way.

You know what meeting more people means – more play dates!

****

LIVE THE LIFE YOU WANT

It was featured in the Derren Brown Showman Tour that the number one regret of most people who were near death was:

> ***I wish I had lived the life I wanted and not the life others wanted for me.***

So many people live the life others wanted for them. Pressure is put onto so many to go down career paths which have been pushed onto them. So many people are working in jobs that they simply hate. If you are in a job that only brings you misery, then it really is time to tell the Universe that you need some new job opportunities sent your way. Take action and find new hobbies to see what makes your heart sing.

Living the life you want means following your heart. Experiment with things to see what brings you joy, what makes you feel alive.

Pursuing your own goals and not the goals of others will always bring satisfaction to your life.

Living the life you want is about knowing what your life purpose is, plus being true to yourself and your own standards.

Pursue your passion to truly live a life of "Pleasure".

Take ownership of your own happiness and well-being. Do not give your power away to others, allowing someone to dictate what you should do with your life.

By living the life you want, you will find you can inspire so many others to do the same. This will create a ripple effect of positive changes in many lives.

Living the life you want isn't always easy to do, but it will be worth it! It may involve making difficult choices that only you can be responsible for. It may involve taking risks, facing criticism and sometimes rejection from others.

Design the life you want.
Rachel Roy

LOVE LIFE

This is also about "Appreciation" (featured in A is for.. chapter). Every morning when you wake up send thanks for your life. Send thanks for this experience. If you are going through a struggle, ask the Universe for a helping hand.

Loving life is about having a zest for life. The determination to find joy in life. Live in the power of now and love the moment.

This means not living in the past and not worrying about the future. All we can ever really experience is the moment of now.

> *Success is loving life and daring to live it.*
> Maya Angelou

Approaching life with a positive and optimistic attitude attracts more positivity into our life. Therefore, boosting our mental and emotional well-being. Achieving greater levels of happiness, resilience and inner peace.

This also enhances relationships we have, as people will be more attracted to your energy. You will be a fun, happy, and inspiring person to be around. Be the person who brings joy to others, and you never get sick of hearing *'you've lifted my spirits'* to which you reply *'It's my pleasure.'* **Be the *'life and soul of the party.'***

The more positive you are means the more success will come your way. You won't see a setback as failure you will see it as a challenge.

Embrace life with passion and enthusiasm. You will then see your life transform into a life full of joy and abundance.

If you have zest and enthusiasm you attract zest and enthusiasm. Life does give back in kind.
Norman Vincent Peale

****

LIVE WITHOUT LIMITS

When you put limits on yourself you limit your potential.

Madonna sang in *'Give it to me'* -

Got no boundaries, got no limits, if there's excitement put me in it.

Live with no limits is one of the most empowering and transformative things you can do in life. Break free from fear and self-doubt. This will give you the strength to pursue your dreams and passions. Be courageous and determined. You will be free to explore your true potential because you won't be held back by fear. This can lead you to find more passions and interests to pursue. You will then have more satisfaction in your life. You will be more resilient and be able to bounce back from any setbacks or failures. You will embrace obstacles as opportunities of growth and learning. By living with no limitations, you will have improved self-confidence. You will push yourself out of your comfort zone and achieve things that you never thought were possible. This will then inspire others.

Living without limits is also about living without labels. I can never understand when people want to put labels on themselves. I don't mean those yellow post-it notes! By not trying to fit into a specific box or label we embrace our uniqueness. Liberate yourself and transform your experience by stop labelling yourself. Be your authentic self. Don't conform to societal expectations or labels.

Live a life truly aligned to your values, beliefs and interests. You will become more empathetic and understanding of others. Nobody should be judged based on their labels or stereotypes. Connect with people on a deeper level rather than trying to fit into our specific roles or labels.

Labels are a form of constraint – break free and live a life as a unique individual and find fulfilment and meaningfulness in all you do. Unleash your uniqueness!

****

LET IT GO

If I had a pound for every time I've heard this song! From the Disney film Frozen 'Let it go' is a powerful message of self-acceptance and empowerment.

> *It's funny how some distance*
> *Makes everything seem small*
> *And the fears that once controlled me*
> *Can't get to me at all.*
> *It's time to see what I can do*
> *To test the limits and break through*
> *No right, no wrong, no rules for me*
> *I'm free. Let it go! Let it go!*

Conveying the message of the importance of letting go of past hurts and fears. With the emphasis on moving forward and embracing the future. A song about the fears that held a person back for so long, but now releasing the memories to allow freedom. No more having to conform to others' expectations. The song is about knowing the power within us all. Embrace your true self in order to live an authentic and fulfilling life.

Encouraging others to be brave and pursue their dreams. Let go of any negative comments from your past that you have allowed to hold you back. I've heard so many stories from people saying that a teacher from their childhood once told them that they would never amount to anything. It's a fact that we often remember criticism and negative comments, but we must learn to let this go!

This song clearly resonated with many people all around the world. It is about the universal experience of overcoming obstacles and embracing our true selves. It's a song about self-acceptance and empowerment. So, stop holding yourself back and 'let it go, let it go'.

****

LISTEN

This is so important. Listen to your inner voice.

How many times does something turn out bad and you wish that you had taken notice of your intuition?

We have all got the power of intuition. It's there to help protect us. Unfortunately, we often dismiss it and carry on regardless. Start taking note and listen to your inner voice.

Intuition is the whisper of the inner soul.
Jiddu Krishnamurti

Listen to others. Many wise words are offered to us over the years, and we sometimes dismiss them. We stubbornly think "I'll do what I want". But how many times have those wise words been spot on. My grandmother used to come out with some very wise words of advice. She used to say, "mark my words, you'll wish you had taken notice of what I'm telling you!". Yes, on reflection, she was very wise indeed.

Listening to others is a skill. We often lose interest if someone doesn't get to the point quick enough. Some people have a habit of jumping to the wrong conclusion because they interrupted before the person has completed their point. If in doubt, ask the person if they have finished before offering your reply. Many of our problems are caused by poor communication skills. It is essential to be able to talk and listen!

Practice active listening – checking in with the person talking by reflecting their words back. Clarifying that you completely understand what they are telling you. This will make the person feel 'listened to' and acknowledged.

By listening to others life experiences and views on the world we also learn so much about the person. This will lead to a greater understanding of the person.

The word 'listen' contains the same letters as the word 'silent'.

E
is for....

ENCOURAGE

Encourage yourself to motivate your dreams into action. Use affirmations on a daily basis to do this.

Encourage yourself, believe in yourself, and love yourself. Never doubt who you are.

By encouraging others to follow their dreams and give them reassurance that you believe in them, will help kickstart them into action!

I read a story about a man who was shot and paralysed. Doctors told him repeatedly that he would never walk again. He spiralled into depression and piled weight on due to lack of exercise and comfort eating. A new doctor approached his bedside one day and told him *"You will walk again"*. The man said he had been told numerous times that he would never walk again. He asked the doctor how he could now be telling him something different. The doctor replied, *"Because I have faith in you"*. The man was then motivated to change his diet and start physio. After many months he was able to walk! A friend of mine told me that she was once in a serious car crash and was told she would never work again by an Occupational Health Doctor. Her dog walker encouraged her to 'reframe' her thinking. *"What if I can get back to work?"* she asked herself. The change in her thinking promoted more positivity, which increased her physical and mental well-being, resulting in her being able to go back to work.

Give constructive criticism / feedback when needed while offering support. Be the light in someone's darkness during difficult times. When someone faces a setback, failure or challenge, give encouragement to carry on and never give up.

> ***Don't give up. 'Cause you have friends***
> ***Don't give up. You're not beaten yet***
> ***Don't give up. I know you can make it good.***
> Don't give up – Peter Gabriel Feat. Kate Bush

****

EXPECTATIONS OF OTHERS LEADS TO DISAPPOINTMENT

Having high expectations of others can often lead to disappointment. Don't create an image in your mind of what we believe someone should be or what they should do. They have their own mind. Your expectations might not align with the reality of what they are or what they want to achieve.

> ***Don't expect too much. It's better to be surprised than disappointed.***

When our expectations are not met, we often feel disappointed or angry. This does not help us achieve happiness.

If you do feel someone has let you down, ask yourself:

> ***Did you expect too much?***
> ***Were your expectations realistic for that person?***

Would that person intentionally hurt you?

To avoid disappointments in the future you need to communicate clearly what you want and / or expect from that person.

It may also be a sign that you need to be more flexible and understanding if something doesn't go as planned.

We all have our own strengths and weaknesses. You may be very confident but someone who lets you down might not have had the confidence to complete the task to your liking. Encouragement needs to come into play not negativity.

Arguments will only lead to the exchange of negative energy. Not having high expectations of others can also promote yourself to be more independent. We often criticise others without ever attempting to do the same thing ourselves!

****

EXPRESS YOURSELF

Over to Madonna again:

Don't go for second best.
You deserve the best in life.

One of my favourite songs is Express Yourself. It also helps that there's a very fit half naked man featured in the video. It's a song about encouraging you to be true to yourself and express their thoughts and feelings without fear of judgement.

Celebrate your uniqueness – we've heard this before haven't we!

We live in a world where conformity is encouraged but we need to keep our individuality and uniqueness. Embrace your own style and identity.

Always be yourself. Express yourself. Have faith in yourself. Do not go out and look for a successful personality and duplicate it.
Bruce Lee

Expressing yourself is also about telling people what you want. If you don't express, it how can people know what you want!

Tell the Universe what you want. The Universe can't set things in motion for you if you don't express your desires! I know many people who have shouted at the Universe. In a moment of utter frustration many people have reported to me that they felt this need to scream and shout, demanding positive changes in their lives. And guess what? It worked every time.

Express yourself don't repress yourself!
Madonna

****

EMOTIONS ARE NOT A SIGN OF WEAKNESS

Some people think showing emotion is a sign of weakness. It is a natural part of being human that we need to release our emotions.

It takes more strength to cry admit defeat.
Madonna – *You'll See*

We must never suppress or ignore our emotions, as this can have a negative effect on our mental health and well-being. We must deal with any issues that cause negative emotions in us. Most times a change in perspective is needed. If we don't deal with the issues that are causing us negativity in life the wound will never heal.

Sometimes the only way to heal is by communication but if one party is stubborn and refuses to talk you have to find another way to deal with the problem. Anger and bitterness will only affect you negatively. Expressing our emotions in a healthy way is very courageous and strengthening.

So, when you feel like a good cry just let it out! Watch a sad movie in order to allow the release of those tears – ***Beaches (Bette Midler Movie)*** makes me cry every time!

But you don't ever, you don't ever have to walk alone
You see, so come on, take my hand
Come on, walk with me
When you're waiting for a voice to come
In the night and there is no one
Don't cha feel like crying?
Don't cha feel like crying, like crying, like crying?
Come on baby, cry to me.
Solomon Burke – Cry to me

If you still need a cry after watching *Beaches*, try watching Machine Gun Preacher or the final episode of Dexter: New Blood Season one!

****

EMPATHY

Being empathetic to others is crucial to help build positive relationships. It helps to connect with people and build trust. The aim is to create a more compassionate and understanding environment to live in.

Empathy works so well because it does not require a solution. It requires only understanding.
John Medina

To be empathetic means to see things from someone else's perspective. To understand their experiences, thoughts and feelings.

Father, Father, Father, help us
Send some guidance from above
'Cause people got me, got me questionin'
Where is the love (love).
The Black Eyed Peas feat. Justin Timberlake

Having empathy for others will also help build stronger relationships. Feeling understood, supported and valued can only benefit your self-esteem. We've all heard the saying 'put yourself in their shoes':

To imagine oneself in the situation or circumstances of another person, so as to understand or empathize with their perspective, opinion, or point of view.

Empathy can also help us solve problems and conflicts. When we empathize with our fellow man it is more difficult to divide people. Let's face it we need to stop being divided.

Not enough love and understanding
We could use some love
To ease these troubled times
Not enough love and understanding.
Cher – Love and Understanding

EMPOWERMENT

You need to gain confidence to excel in all areas of your life. When you ooze self-confidence, you open yourself up to more opportunities. You will have greater self-esteem and independence. As Katy Perry sings in 'Roar':

> *I used to bite my tongue and hold my breath*
> *Scared to rock the boat and make a mess*
> *So I sat quietly, agreed politely*
> *I guess that I forgot I had a choice*
> *I let you push me past the breaking point*
> *I stood for nothing, so I fell for everything ......*
> *Get ready 'cause I've had enough*
> *I see it all, I see it now*
> *I got the eye of the tiger, a fighter*
> *Dancing through the fire*
> *'Cause I am a champion, and you're gonna hear me roar.*

If you don't feel like you have confidence, then simply fake it. Invent a new persona for yourself. Many singers and comedians are completely different from their on-stage persona. Don't hold yourself back through lack of confidence or shyness.

> *Don't fake it till you make it. Fake it till you become it.*
> Amy Cuddy

Develop a sense of self-awareness and positive self-image. Recognize your strengths and weaknesses. Build on your strengths and address your weaknesses. Set yourself goals.

Develop skills and knowledge relevant to your long-term goals and aspirations. Empowerment is about taking action. If there are areas in your life that make you unhappy then take charge and make the changes you can.

****

EXERCISE

Instead of sitting around worrying about a situation go for a walk or run. Regular exercise has so many benefits. It helps us maintain a healthy weight which in turn makes us feel more confident with our body image. It gives us energy. Exercise can be very therapeutic when dealing with problems.

Sometimes a workout is all the therapy you need.

By joining an exercise class, walking / running group, or any other form of physical activity group, you will also meet more people. Extending your support network which will benefit your mental health.

Regular exercise can also reduce the risks of various health issues.

You will have more energy needed for when you want to play out with your friends!

Exercise will reduce levels of stress and improve your sleep. Especially if you had a really good session in the gym!

Let's get physical, physical
I wanna get physical
Let's get into physical.
Olivia Newton John

Exercise and eating healthy can also have a positive impact on your bank balance. Eating healthy will mean you will actually eat less as some junk food actually makes you hungrier – a well-known crisp springs to mind – once you pop you can't stop! Drinking more water can also help you eat less. Walking or running instead of using the car will save you money on petrol. Having an active lifestyle rather than sitting in front of the television all day will also save you money on your energy bills.

A
is for....

APPRECIATE

One of the keys to manifesting successfully is appreciation.

By showing the Universe you appreciate what you have, you will be rewarded with more of what you want. I asked the Universe for a lottery win not so long ago. I won a lucky dip later that night. My immediate thought was *'Universe that wasn't what I meant.'* I then realised I needed to thank the Universe. I imagined giving a child a bag of sweets and then the child declaring *'I wanted a bigger bag!'* Well, I would think that child was a spoilt brat. And guess what? I wouldn't give that child another bag of sweets.

I believe the Universe thinks the same. Why would it reward you for being ungrateful?

Appreciation is about focusing on the good things in your life and being grateful.

It's a lovely feeling to be appreciated. We have all experienced a feeling of annoyance to somebody for not appreciating our efforts. Lift someone's spirit by acknowledging appreciation. You will make them feel valued, and respected. This can only help build stronger relationships.

A person who feels appreciated will always do more than expected.

The law of attraction promotes us to focus on positive aspects of our lives, therefore attract more positive things into our lives.

Remember to show appreciation whenever you can. A text message, an email, or a Thank you card doesn't take much effort when you think about it. A small gesture like "Thank you" can make someone feel appreciated and loved.

****

ASK FOR HELP

Never suffer in silence. Confide in a family member or friend if you need help. If you have nobody to talk to or don't feel you can raise a sensitive subject with someone you know talk to the Universe. Use the power of prayer and send requests for help. Talk to your guardian angel or a loved one in the spirit world.

You are never alone. Asking for help is not a weakness. When you ask for help you open yourself up to advice from others which you may previously never have thought of. Gaining options and insight to help face challenges and overcome obstacles. Asking for help shows others that you are open-minded and willing to grow and learn. The power of prayer is undeniable. Thoughts are living things. Send your thoughts to the Universe and help will come.

I know a few people who have sent prayers at times in their lives when they have needed support and friendship. The Universe always answered their prayers and as if by magic people came into their lives offering the support they needed. I believe we all have a guardian angel.

A few years ago, my partner and I were woken up by a dog barking at 5am every morning. This went on for weeks and as you can imagine we were fed up with this unwanted wake up call. We didn't know which home the dog belonged to, so couldn't directly complain to anyone. One evening while reading a spiritual magazine I read about Guardian Angels. It stated that if you had a problem with someone and couldn't feel you could talk to them directly you could ask your guardian angel to talk to their guardian angel. The guardian angels would then work together to work the problem out. Yes, I know what you are thinking.... Bizarre! But what did we have to lose? I went to bed that night and said, 'Can my guardian angel tell dog owners guardian angel to not let the dog out at 5 o'clock in the morning anymore?' Next morning, we were woken again by the dog barking! However, when we checked the time, it was 7 o'clock. The dog never woke us up again at 5 o'clock, so technically it worked!

****

ANXIETY MUST BE AVOIDED

Eliminate as much anxiety and stress from your life. Obviously, there will be times in life when we experience stress. The important thing is to be able to eliminate it or reduce it as quickly as possible. Chronic anxiety and stress can impact on our health and well-being. It can affect our ability to think clearly and rationally. Affecting decision making and generally disrupting the flow of our daily lives.

Sometimes you just need to take a deep breath.

You need to develop coping strategies and stress management techniques to eliminate stress from life. Ways to do this include practising mindfulness, exercise, healthy sleep patterns. It is also vital to seek support from family and friends. Regular meditation can also be a useful addition to our daily lives to maintain calmness and relaxation.

Put aside all anxious thoughts and be at peace.
Francis De Sales

Over the last three years (2020 – 2023) I found watching mainstream media and the news was causing me anxiety. The attention-grabbing headlines on the front pages of the daily newspaper would also trigger an anxious feeling inside me. I could not understand and still cannot comprehend the intentions of mainstream media, which seemed to want to cause fear and terror to the general public. I turned the television off and do not need to look at newspaper headlines. This simple act eliminated anxiety from my life. I cannot recommend it enough!

If it's out of your control, don't let it control you.
****

ANGEL GUIDANCE

I believe in the power of angels. Guiding and protecting our journey on this earth plane. Many people believe in these spiritual beings that communicate with us through signs and symbols.

By opening your mind and learning about angel numbers you can gain much needed peace of mind. Sequences of numbers such as 111, 222, 333, 444, 555,

666, 777, 888, 999 have specific meanings and messages for us. There are many websites explaining the meaning of angel numbers. Here is a brief explanation of these numbers:

111 Embrace New Beginnings
222 You're on a righteous path
333 It's time to get balanced,
444 Sending Signs Of Encouragement
555 Associated with change.
666 Asks you to redirect your energy so you'll thrive
777 Your spirit and soul are in alignment.
888 Is all about abundance
999 Associated with completion

There are many more explanations for these numbers. There is so much more about angel numbers, I urge to do further research!
Many people also believe angels can communicate with us through our intuition, dreams and synchronicities.
The belief in angels can bring comfort to many people, therefore bring peace and calmness to our lives.
Are angels real? Are we deluding ourselves? Is the power of the mind what really gets us through difficult situations? Who knows? But I am happy to say the sense of protection that encompasses you by the belief of angels is a wondrous thing.

****

ACTS OF KINDNESS

This really is an important principle to follow. By doing an act of kindness for another brings a happy feeling to yourself.

How beautiful a day can be when kindness touches it.
George Elliston

It feels great to know you have done something for someone that has been appreciated. The act of helping another human being increases our level of happiness and well-being. Doing something kind activates the pleasure centres of our brain and releases feel-good hormones. This reduces our stress levels. Doing good for others will also strengthen our relationships.

Sometimes it takes only one act of kindness and caring to change a person's life.
Jackie Chan

Whenever I think about acts of kindness I think of the film "Pay it Forward." The film stars Kevin Spacey, Helen Hunt and Haley Joel Osment. It tells the story of a young boy set a task by his schoolteacher. He has to think of an idea that could have a positive impact on the world. He sets out to change the world by doing three good deeds for others. Those three people will then pay it forward and so on. This film highlights the ripple effect of positivity and generosity.

Sometimes you can't pay it back, so you just have to pay it forward.
Randy Pausch

Most people appreciate an offer of help such as holding a door open for them. Or, letting them in front of you at the queue in a supermarket, when they've only got a loaf of bread and you've got a trolley load of food!

No act of kindness no matter how small is ever wasted.
Aesop

AGREE TO DISAGREE

One of the most important principles in my opinion. By agreeing to disagree you eliminate the escalation to arguments. One of the most important things you can learn is that you need to respect other people's opinions to maintain healthy relationships.

People have different opinions – **Accept it!** The easiest thing to do when someone has a different opinion to you is label the person. However, we don't want to live with labels so don't use labels on others. By agreeing to disagree you show respect for another opinion. This doesn't mean you believe in it or accept it in your reality. It means you are capable of respecting others.

We don't need to share the same opinions as others, but we need to be respectful.
Taylor Swift

You show maturity and understanding when you can simply say we can agree to disagree. This also shows open-mindedness and empathy. Showing consideration for other beliefs but being able to stand by your own in a compassionate way. By removing the possibility of an argument, you promote a sense of peace and harmony.

Madonna sums it up perfectly in her song 'Borrowed time':

Do we need to start a war?
Do we need to take a side?
Doesn't matter underneath it all
'Cause we're only here to love.

ANALYSE AND APPLY LOGIC

In other words, never stop questioning. Ask yourself *'Does it make sense?'* Don't act irrational when a situation takes you by surprise. Use logic to decide how the situation can be resolved. Using logic is all also about thinking critically about the world around us.

If something doesn't make sense, then you need to dig a little deeper to find out what the real cause of the situation is.

The quicker you can apply logic, the faster you can solve the problem. This leads to less stress and more time to focus on other areas of your life. Ask yourself:

How can you be good at solving problems if you aren't able to identify the real problem?
Do you blindly accept any information given to you?
Do you believe everything people tell you?

Make your life so much easier by taking the time to analyse things. This leads you to make better informed decisions and avoid making mistakes. Check information you have been given is correct and complete. It's a fact of life that most people tell lies. In most cases they will be small lies, but they are still lies. By listening and analysing what people tell you, you will be able to decipher if someone is being honest with you. Let's face it most relationships or friendships break down through people not being honest with each other. Consider training in Statement Analysis. If you want more information, please look up Peter Hyatt on YouTube. One important rule to remember is never assume anything. When someone tries to dupe us, they will often answer a question with vagueness. Hoping to leave you with an assumption of something. Always clarify the answer. Ask yourself:

Did they answer the question?
Was it vague?
Are you satisfied you have all the information you require?

S
is for....

STICK IT OUT

Inspired by the Right Said Fred Comic Relief song.
Sticking it out is basically never giving up. Persevere with challenges and setbacks. It's about the mindset of never taking no for an answer. You know what your goal is and you're going to keep pushing.

Stay Strong,
Stay Positive,
And never give up.
Roy T. Bennett

This demonstrates your resilience. When we face a setback the easiest thing to do is give up. If you really want something that you know is going to make you happy then giving up is never an option.

When you do achieve your goal, it feels like a greater success because you had to work harder for it. It shows your determination and commitment.

When you stick it out and succeed you can inspire others to pursue their own goals and dreams.

Watch the film 'Bank of Dave' the story of David Fishwick. He is such a charismatic, happy man who never gives up. His story is inspirational and a true example of perseverance.

STAND IN YOUR POWER

Standing in your power means having a strong sense of self-confidence, self-worth, and personal authority. Owning and asserting your own beliefs, values, boundaries and being willing to speak up. Take action to defend them when necessary. Be more authentic and true to yourself. Show confidence in your beliefs and values.

You will be taken more seriously and respected by others when you show confidence and assertiveness.

Your power to manifest the life you want is within.

Surround yourself with positive people and you will manifest more positivity.

Standing in your power is also about standing in your truth.

Be honest with yourself. Don't try to live up to other people's expectations. This will never lead you to happiness.

Standing in your truth doesn't mean forcing your beliefs or values on others. It doesn't matter what other people think of you. Not everyone will like you or agree with your views. Just have a look online to see the variety of opinions about celebrities' lives. The nastiness and vileness out there is not something I want in my reality. I stand in my truth, but I do not get involved with joining online conversations.

Be honest about who you are but be prepared that not everyone will like who you are. Not everyone will share your views. Stay true to who you are without causing yourself negativity.

Do not give your energy to people who try to bring negative energy to your life. By standing in your truth, you will attract people and opportunities that align with your values. Building a strong network of people who trust and respect you.

It can also inspire others and stand by their values and beliefs.

****

SILENCE IS A VIRTUE

Sometimes it's better to say nothing to avoid doing more harm than good.

Silence is a source of great strength.
Lao Tzu

Remaining silent can sometimes be seen as a sign of strength and wisdom. It also demonstrates self-control. Avoid unnecessary conflict or drama by keeping out of a situation. Only you can make the judgement in each situation about what to do for the best.

By learning how to analyse a situation you will then become wise as to when to say something and when to say nothing!

I remember once asking a friend advice about a situation. It was one of those times where I didn't know whether to get involved and was at a loss for the words I would use. My friend (a fellow Geordie) replied: *"Dawn, When in doubt, say nowt!"*. I followed his advice. It mustn't have been an important problem as I can't recall what the situation was now, or the people involved! His words always stuck in my mind though.

Some people think staying silent means you are sitting on the fence and afraid of confrontation. I understand this point, however, life is full of contradiction and people are complex characters. Every situation is different, and I don't feel anything is black or white. It really comes down to being able to assess the problem and the people involved before deciding the way forward.

Whatever you choose to do, stay calm and rational. Treat others with respect and do not escalate the situation with negativity.

Words are very unnecessary
They can only do harm.
Depeche Mode – Enjoy the Silence

It's a case of choosing your battles carefully in life!
****

<u>SMILE</u>

Wouldn't it be a lovely sight, to walk down the street and see everyone smile at each other. Smiling at each other improves your mood. It lifts feelings of stress and anxiety. When you smile your brain releases endorphins. These are chemicals that promote the feelings of happiness and well-being. We need human connection, and a smile lets people know we are friendly and approachable.

Use your smile to change the world, don't let the world change your smile.

When you smile at someone you are communicating you are open and receptive to conversation. This can lead to forming new friendships which can lead to more play dates! I remember meeting my lovely friend Lisa at a Madonna concert. She was staying at the same hotel. After the concert, Gary and I sat in the hotel bar, knocking back a few glasses of wine trying to get over the excitement of seeing Madonna close up. This lady walked in the bar (wait, this sounds like the beginning of a joke) and smiled at me. I smiled back and she approached our table and introduced herself. We then spent hours talking about how much we loved Madonna. Years later she confessed to me that she's not really a people person and her actions that night were completely out of character. She remembers me smiling at her which gave her the confidence to come and talk to us. Whoever smiled first I'm glad it happened, otherwise I would never have met my wonderful 'mate' Lisa. Smiling can also have a positive impact on our health. So, go on brighten someone's day by flashing those lovely gnashers of yours. When you smile at someone it is very likely they will smile back. Creating a positive atmosphere where people feel happier and more positive.

A smile is the prettiest thing you can wear.
****

SING AND DANCE

Hey, Mr. DJ, put a record on
I wanna dance with my baby
Music makes the people come together.
Madonna – Music

Singing and dancing, what's not to love? Two activities that make us feel great and are beneficial to our health and well-being, both physical and mental. Have fun and improve your health. Singing and dancing can reduce stress and promote relaxation. Another principle to follow which allows our body to release endorphins. Both these activities boost self-esteem and happiness.

You could make one of your play dates a trip to the pub for a karaoke night. Never under-estimate how quickly you can turn your mood around by playing an upbeat song. Songs have the power to transport you back in time to happy memories. So, whenever you feel blue, stick a tune you love on and pick yourself up and get back in the race. Wait, that sounds familiar!

Of course, you could also join a choir if you have a love of singing. You might meet more wonderful people to make play dates with.

I'm a child of the eighties so I remember creating mix tapes. Trying to record your favourite hits from the weekly chart run down on the radio without getting the DJ's voice on the recording! It truly was a knack which I am proud to say I did finally master.

Music is one of the things I am most grateful in life. I have attended many concerts and am lucky to say I have probably seen all the acts I have ever wanted to see. Obviously, seeing Madonna eleven times in concert has brought me the most pleasure. I very nearly touched her as she walked down the aisle past me. I put my hand out only for her security man to hit my hand out of the way!

So, remember when you ever feel down stick a tune on that lifts your spirits or takes your mind back to a time of happiness.

****

SEEK KNOWLEDGE

One of the biggest lessons you can learn is that you don't know everything.

Seeking knowledge is about being open to learning and opening our minds to different topics.

Seeking knowledge is like opening doors. And I know the doors are everywhere.
George St-Pierre

Does it make sense? Comes into play here again. Research is the key. There is so much disinformation in the media and online sometimes it's hard to know what to believe. If something intrigues you do more research!

Getting in tune with your inner power and trusting your intuition also comes into play here. We often ignore our gut feeling and blindly believe something someone tells us. Our gut feeling is telling us 'Something doesn't add up here', but we don't want to hurt someone's feeling by questioning them.

Knowledge is Power

An important aspect of seeking knowledge is also to be of help to each other. We can share our knowledge to help someone else's journey in life become a little easier. That's why I'm sharing this knowledge in this book – I want to make your life so much more pleasurable!

A man I follow on YouTube is called Paul Marles. I have learnt so much from Paul simply by watching his videos. It has opened so many opportunities for me.

So go on, knock on the door of knowledge!

****

SELF-CARE

It is vital you make time for yourself. So many people spend their days fulfilling the needs of others and don't spend time on themselves. Find time to meditate, exercise and engage in activities that bring you joy.

An empty lantern provides no light. Self-care is the fuel that allows your light to shine brightly.

By looking after your needs, you will be a happier person. You will feel healthier. Time needs to be set aside for your needs on a daily basis. Do not neglect yourself. You are not selfish for putting your needs first. I speak to many people who are suffering stress in their lives. I always recommend setting aside 10 minutes a day to meditate. *"I haven't got time for that"* they often reply. What they are saying is that they don't value themselves enough to prioritise their own needs.

Self-care is also about loving yourself. Many people have trouble maintaining a healthy relationship because they probably don't have a great relationship with themselves. To say you love yourself does not mean you are obsessed with yourself. It's about knowing and accepting you are worthy of love and respect.

You will be more resilient when you suffer challenges in life.

You will be better equipped to have healthy and fulfilling relationships.

Loving yourself means better mental health. Eliminate negative self-talk, self-doubt and self-criticism. This will help lower levels of stress, anxiety and depression.

By being happy within your life you will celebrate more pleasure and fulfilment.

Affirmations are an excellent way to show yourself love. Practice self-love by being kind to yourself and not putting up with second best.

U
is for....

UNDERSTAND

Having empathy for others leads to greater understanding.

Seek first to understand, then to be understood.
Stephen R Covey

By having a deeper understanding of someone we can adapt how we communicate. We will be aware of their thoughts and beliefs. Remember we must respect each other even when our opinions differ.

By acknowledging different viewpoints, it is easier to work together to find solutions that will meet all party's needs.

How can you resolve a disagreement with someone if you can't understand their point?

The key to resolving issues requires communication. Talk about the issues. Listen to the other point of view. Once you understand the reasons behind the issue, then you can use negotiation to resolve in favour of both (or all) parties. ***Understanding is deeper than knowledge. There are many people who know you, but there are very few who understand you.***

UNIVERSAL LAW

The one law of the Universe we should all follow is Do No Harm. Can you imagine the peace in the world this would manifest?
Do you believe in Karma?

> *I believe in karma, what you give is what you get returned.*
> Savage Garden – Affirmation

How you treat others will always come back to you. I am a strong believer in Karma and personally I don't think you can escape it.

> **Karma is the Universal law of cause and effect you reap what you sow.**

Do No Harm is basically a fundamental principle of encouraging peace, harmony and well-being to all. It's about being mindful of how actions can affect our lives and the lives of others. Surely it makes more sense to cause a ripple effect of positivity and happiness than negativity. Doing good deeds for other people brings you so much joy, I really can't understand people who seem to go out of their way to hurt people. I then came to understand that *hurt people, hurt people.*
I recommend all readers to watch Mark Passio's lecture on Natural law as it explains so much. Some people think that if they do something bad because they followed orders protects them against Karma. This is Mark Passio's opinion on this viewpoint:

> **The order-follower always bears more moral culpability than the order-giver, because the order-follower is the one who actually performed the action,**

and in taking such action, actually brought the resultant harm into physical manifestation. Order-following is the pathway to every form of evil and chaos in our world. It should never be seen as a 'virtue' by anyone who considers themselves a moral human being. Order followers have ultimately been personally responsible and morally culpable for every form of slavery and every single totalitarian regime that has ever existed upon the face of the earth.

****

USE WORDS WISELY

Never under-estimate how powerful your words are. Words can uplift and inspire. Words can tear down and destroy. Choose your words carefully. Be mindful of how your words can hurt another.

Words are like weapons they wound sometimes.
Cher – If I could turn back time

When you want to manifest it is important you use your words wisely. It is also important to use present-tense language when talking to the Universe. So, instead of saying *"I want to be happy"* you need to state, *"I am happy and fulfilled in my life right now."* Through repeating positive affirmations like this you focus your thoughts and energy of the desired outcome. You are confirming to the Universe you trust you have been granted what you desire.

Many people tell the Universe what they want then add *"I hope I get what I want."* All the Universe has heard is doubt, which then cancels out what you want. You must speak like you already have what you desire.

By using words that make people feel good about themselves raises their vibration and yours. This will then lead to more positive things happening.

Don't focus on someone's weakness when you could praise their strengths. Insulting someone will only create negativity and more than likely cause the other person to insult you!

Words are powerful – and your mind is listening.
Marisa Peer

****

UNLOCK YOUR POTENTIAL

The main reason people are unhappy is normally due to not pursuing a passion or finding a passion at all. We all have strengths and weaknesses.

A sense of purpose is essential for our well-being and happiness.

Give me a sense of purpose
A real sense of purpose now.
The Pretenders – A sense of Purpose

We all like to be of value and help to others – well most of us anyway! Many people who can't find employment choose to volunteer with charities. This can help people feel like they are contributing to a meaningful cause. This also helps get them experience to enable them to gain employment.

Don't sit around and feel you have no purpose.

One person cannot help everyone, but everyone can help one person.

Set yourself goals everyday this gives your day purpose. This gives you a reason to wake up each morning.

Making a positive impact on the world gives you a feeling of passion and enthusiasm which will bring you happiness.

So many people are in employment that makes then unhappy. They are not using their full potential.

Do you want to learn a musical instrument?

Do you want to study?

Do you want to be more creative?

Do you want to turn your hobby into full-time employment?

Well, **what are you waiting for?** Stop making excuses and unlock your potential. If you don't try you will never know.

And, no you are never too old to try something new!

****

UNCLUTTERED LIFESTYLE

Did you ever have a friendship or relationship break down and you realise you never want to see that person again? The sight of the person brings you feelings of anger and bitterness. Firstly, delete their number from your phone. You don't want any abusive messages that will raise your anger levels.

As I unclutter my life, I free myself to answer the callings of my soul.
Dr Wayne Dyer

Do you know someone who drains your energy? We all have at least one person in our lives who use you as a counsellor. That's fine, we are here to support each other. However, there is always the person who offloads onto you, with no intention of changing their life they just want a moan. They leave, leaving you with a splitting headache and completely drained.

I'm not saying eliminate these people from your life, but you need to learn how to protect yourself. Don't waste your energy trying to give advice if you can tell they have no intention of taking action. My advice is to support by listening but don't let their words impact on you. I have had a few friends who have been in abusive relationships. I used to get so angry on their behalf when they would cry to me about how much they hated their lives. It would frustrate me that they would put up with this when I could see they deserved so much more.

Letting go of physical clutter also declutters mind and soul.

April Williams

Bad energy can also be attached to belongings. I recommend a regular declutter. A cluttered home can represent a cluttered mind. By clearing out items that you don't need can be a very liberating experience.

****

UMPIRE YOUR OWN GAME

Be the umpire of your game of life. Set your own rules and moral codes.

Ethics is a code of values which guide our choices and actions and determine the purpose and course of our lives.

Ayn Rand

Whenever I think of moral codes I think of Dexter Morgan. 'Dexter' is my favourite TV programme.

Dexter has his own code that he follows precisely. *"Am I a good person doing 'bad' things or a bad person doing 'good' things?" Dexter once asked himself!*

Never let the unacceptable become acceptable.
Lesley Cassidy

It is important for you to set your own moral codes of what is acceptable and unacceptable. What might be acceptable to you will not necessarily be acceptable to someone else. When starting a new relationship, we need to set our ground rules so we know we are both on the same page. It's about compatibility.

It also sets boundaries and standards. I know this contradicts Madonna singing *'Got no boundaries'*, but we've got to be realistic here. If you haven't got boundaries - set some - as people will take advantage of you.

Remember only you can set your moral codes. Stand by your principles. Of course, over time your moral codes may change due to experiences in our lives. Our viewpoints on different issues change as we mature and / or gain more knowledge about a topic.

Avoid toxic relationships by maintaining a strong moral code of what is unacceptable to you.

A man without ethics is a wild beast loosed upon the world.
Albert Camus

****

UNITY

When we work together, I believe the magic truly happens. **United we stand, divided we fall.**

When we show support for each other we feel empowered and stronger. I believe we are living through a very challenging time in history and the need for unity is greater than ever. That's why I'm writing this book! As humanity we need to lift our vibration and eliminate fear and negativity. Love is the greatest power. We have allowed humanity to be divided for so long – it's time to realise that division is not the answer it is the problem.

What we need is not division….it's love and wisdom and compassion toward one another.
Robert F Kennedy

Divide and conquer needs to be eliminated for the good of our earth.

When the world, leaves you feeling blue
You can count on me, I will be there for you
When it seems, all your hopes and dreams
Are a million miles away, I will reassure you
We've got to all stick together
Good friends are there for each other
Never, ever forget that I got you
And you got me.
S Club 7 – Reach

R
is for....

REVENGE IS NEVER THE ANSWER

Holding onto any negative emotion is not beneficial for you, physically or mentally. Being successful and happy is the best revenge. The point is you will be enjoying your success and creating happy memories, that you forget all about the person or situation you once focused anger and bitterness on.

No man heals himself by wounding another.

If you are living your life wanting revenge, you are giving your power away. The person your revenge and anger is focused on has power over your emotions. It's time to decide - are you going to be bitter or be better!

An eye for an eye will only make the whole world blind.
Mahatma Gandhi

Revenge can often lead to a cycle of negativity and a ripple effect of anger and hurt.
Letting go of bitterness and anger doesn't mean you forgive the actions of another. The need to free yourself from the pain and hurt is essential for your well-being.

If you spend your time hoping someone will suffer the consequences for what they did to your heart, then

you're allowing them to hurt you a second time in your mind.
Shannon L. Alder

Practising the Power of now (living in the moment of now) will help you focus your attention on your present situation and experience. Meaning you are not thinking of the past.

****

REFLECTION

Yes, I know reflection isn't living in the now. However, positive reflection can help us build our self-confidence and self-esteem.

When looking back and reflecting on what you have achieved in life, you will then have a feeling of satisfaction and belief that you can continue to prosper.

Self reflection is the school of wisdom.
Baltasar Gracian

This can also benefit relationships. When someone disappoints or hurt us reflect on their past behaviour. If past experiences with this person have been positive why let one moment of disappointment ruin a healthy relationship?

Do you need to change your perspective? Was their intention to hurt you?

Be a reflection of what you'd like to see in others.

****

RESPECT

Respect is crucial for maintaining healthy relationships and living a fulfilling life. By showing respect for ourselves and others, we can build trust, promote empathy, reduce conflict, enhance self-esteem and foster a sense of community. When we treat others with kindness and dignity, we create a safe and inclusive environment where everyone can thrive and flourish.

Respect yourself and others will respect you.
Confucius

Respect for yourself is important for helping you establish what is acceptable and unacceptable to you. Treat others as you would like to be treat yourself.
****

REFUSE TO LIVE IN FEAR

To live a true life of pleasure you cannot allow fear to hold you back. There are many things we can be fearful of in this material world. One of the main things that holds us back is fear from what others think of us. What will other people think if I do this? Who cares! Live the life you want instead of trying to live up to other peoples' expectations.

The greatest prison people live in is the fear of what other people think.
David Icke

Fear of failure is another common hold back. You'll never know if something will work out if you don't try. Again, it's all about perspective. You haven't failed you have simply found out that something doesn't work.

Everything you have ever wanted is on the other side of fear.

Fear can bring feelings of panic and anxiety which can only be bad for our health.

It's time to reclaim your power and eliminate fear in all forms!

> ***Fear is the most subtle and destructive of all human diseases. Fear kills dream and hope.***
> Les Brown

****

RIDE THE ROLLER-COASTER

Inspired by the song 'Life is a roller-coaster' by Ronan Keating.

I must admit I'm not a great fan of Ronan Keating. I'm sure he's a nice enough bloke but his music isn't really my cup of tea. I'm into the hard stuff like, oh I don't know, Bucks Fizz and The Nolans. I'm joking! However, I do appreciate a good song when I hear one. 'Life is a Roller-coaster' is an upbeat song to get you singing along. Conveying the message that life can be full of ups and downs, twists and turns, etc.

> ***Life is a roller-coaster, you've just got to ride it.***
> Ronan Keating

However, we sometimes have to go with the flow of the ride. It's about the importance of being able to adapt to change. The song promotes the importance of enjoying the journey of life, appreciate the good times and ride out the hard times. It's about supporting each other. It's a song about perseverance and optimism.

I also love this quote by Bill Hicks:

> ***The world is like a ride in an amusement park, and when you choose to go on it you think it's real because that's how powerful our minds are. The ride goes up and down, around and around, it has thrills and chills,***

and it's very brightly coloured, and it's very loud, and it's fun for a while. Many people have been on the ride a long time, and they begin to wonder, "Hey, is this real, or is this just a ride?" And other people have remembered, and they come back to us and say, "Hey, don't worry; don't be afraid, ever, because this is just a ride.

****

RAZZLE DAZZLE

Inspired by the song from Chicago the musical:

Give 'em the old razzle dazzle
Razzle dazzle 'em
Give 'em an act with lots of flash in it
And the reaction will be passionate.

Always give your best. Set out to impress. Let your uniqueness shine through.

Oh, I haven't got the confidence to put myself forward, I hear you mutter. Have you ever heard the phrase 'Fake it till you make it?' Embrace and love your uniqueness. Do your best whatever you do:

Whatever you decide to do
Just give it your best, and that will be fine.
Dennis Locorierre – Shine Son

****

RETRAIN YOUR BRAIN

This could possibly be the hardest principle to follow. Unlearning what you think you know. Sometimes we get so steadfast with our beliefs we refuse to see something from a different perspective.

You can't live a positive life with a negative mind.

We get set in our ways and become a creature of habit. Even if those habits are impacting our lives in a negative way.

> ***Being more positive just takes practice. You can retrain your mind to see the best possibilities in everything.***
> Bryant Mcgill

I recently discovered Marisa Peer. She is amazing. Her videos on YouTube are life changing. In one of her videos, she explains how our brains like what is familiar and dislikes what is unfamiliar. Changing your mindset is all about training your brain to make the unfamiliar become the familiar.

So the key is repetition of these positive visualisations. It takes repeating and practising something twenty-one times over twenty-one days for the brain to create new neurological habit pathways, and in turn it takes twenty-one days for those pathways to begin to diminish if you cease the actions.
Marisa Peer

E
is for....

As we've already covered the letter E in chapter 3 I have decided that this E in the word Pleasure stands for:

EXPECT THE UNEXPECTED

"Expect the unexpected" is a phrase that suggests that you should always be prepared for surprises or unforeseen circumstances. It implies that life is unpredictable and that unexpected things can happen at any time, no matter how well-prepared we are.

This expression can be applied to various situations in life, from everyday situations to major life events. Have an open mind, be adaptable, and embrace change.

In essence, "expect the unexpected" is a reminder that life is full of surprises. We should be ready to face them with a positive attitude with a willingness to learn and grow. It encourages individuals to be resilient, stay optimistic and seize opportunities, even in the face of unexpected challenges.

The more the world is changing
The more it stays the same
Life is full of small surprises
It's a never ending game
If nothing is impossible
Will you believe your eyes
If the unexpected brings a smile
That's a big surprise
Surprise, surprise, the unexpected hits you between the eyes
The unpredictable, that's the surprise you see, surprise! Surprise!
Cilla Black – Surprise Surprise

****

The Soundtrack

I had the idea to create this fun playlist for you because I love music. Each song is relevant to the corresponding principle. Please take the time to listen to the songs listed below or look up the lyrics.

PLEASE YOURSELF	My Way – Frank Sinatra
PRAISE	Praise You – Fatboy Slim
PERSPECTIVE	Always Look On The Bright Side Of Life – Monty Python
PACK IT	Moving On Up – M People
PLAY OUT	Get The Party Started – Pink
PERSONAL RESPONSIBILITY	Man In The Mirror – Michael Jackson
PRIORITISE	Get Happy – Judy Garland
LAUGH	Happiness – Ken Dodd
LEARN	You Live You Learn – Alanis Morisette
LIVE THE LIFE YOU WANT	Live Your Life Be Free – Belinda Carlisle
LOVE LIFE	Living In The Moment – Jason Mraz
LIVE WITHOUT LIMITS	Give It To Me – Madonna
LET IT GO	Let It Go – From Frozen
LISTEN	Listen – Beyonce
ENCOURAGE	Roar – Katy Perry
EXPECTATIONS OF OTHERS…..	Power – Little Mix
EXPRESS YOURSELF	Express Yourself – Madonna
EMOTIONS ARE NOT A SIGN …..	You'll See – Madonna

EMPATHY	Love Resurrection – Alison Moyet
EMPOWERMENT	I Will Survive – Gloria Gaynor
EXERCISE	Physical – Olivia Newton-John
APPRECIATE	Thank You – Dido
ASK FOR HELP	Help! - The Beatles
ANXIETY MUST BE..	Don't Worry Be Happy – Bobby McFerrin
ANGEL GUIDANCE	I Have A Dream – Abba
ACTS OF KINDNESS	Count On Me – Bruno Mars
AGREE TO DISAGREE	We Just Disagree – Dave Mason
ANALYSE	The Logical Song – Supertramp
STICK IT OUT	Stick It Out – Right Said Fred
STAND IN YOUR POWER	Happy – Matt Hoy
SILENCE IS A VIRTUE	Patience – Take That
SMILE	Smile – Nat King Cole
SING AND DANCE	I'm In The Mood For Dancing – The Nolans
SEEK KNOWLEDGE	Knowledge Is Power – The Ethopians
SELF-CARE	It's All About You – McFly
UNDERSTAND	Love And Understanding – Cher
UNIVERSAL LAW	Affirmation – Savage Garden
USE WORDS WISELY	Words – The Bee Gees
UNLOCK YOUR POTENTIAL	Sense Of Purpose – The Pretenders
UNITY	Lean On Me – Bill Withers
UMPIRE	The Name Of The Game – Abba
UNCLUTTERED LIFESTYLE	Shake It Off – Taylor Swift
REVENGE IS NEVER THE ANSWER	Since U Been Gone – Kelly Clarkson
REFLECTION	Don't Stop Believing – Journey

RESPECT	Respect – Aretha Franklin
REFUSE TO LIVE IN FEAR	You're The Voice – John Farnham
RIDE THE ROLLER-COASTER	Life Is A Roller-Coaster – Ronan Keating
RAZZLE DAZZLE	Razzle Dazzle – From Chicago
RETRAIN YOUR BRAIN	Thinking Out Loud – Ed Sheeran
EXPECT THE UNEXPECTED	Surprise Surprise – Cilla Black

I hope you like my tracklist and I now encourage you to create your own.

PART TWO

<u>EXERCISES</u>

Now you have a basic understanding of what each principle means we can now move onto the hard work – Applying these principles to your daily lives.

I ask you to consider all the principles and complete all the exercises in this book. You may want to grab a notebook so you can make additional notes.

Here we go….

EXERCISE #1

Your first exercise is to choose one principle from each letter to create your list of 8 principles for daily life. If you don't like any of my choices, please feel free to create your own.

P _____
L _____
E _____
A _____
S _____
U _____
R _____
E _____

....
....
....
....
....
....
....
....
....
....

EXERCISE #2

Write a list of ten things that bring you pleasure. For example, it could be meeting up with friends for a meal, finding time to pursue a hobby, etc.

It could be something as simple as watching a film with a nice cup of hot chocolate by yourself.

The important part of this exercise is for you to focus on yourself and what makes you feel happy. Don't worry about how you will find the time to do these things – we will come to that part later!

So, it's time now to sit in silence and contemplate what activities or things bring you pleasure:

1 _____
2 _____
3 _____
4 _____
5 _____
6 _____
7 _____
8 _____
9 _____
10 _____

EXERCISE #3

It's time to focus on yourself. Congratulate yourself on five things you have achieved in life:

1 _____
2 _____
3 _____
4 _____
5 _____

EXERCISE #4

Now, focus on five people you know. Write the names down of five people you know who you feel deserve praise for what they have achieved in life. Would you like to thank someone for inspiring you or helping you through life?

1 _____
2 _____
3 _____
4 _____
5 _____

EXERCISE #5

What current problems or setbacks do you feel you are facing at the moment?

1 _____
2 _____
3 _____
4 _____
5 _____

A good way to see things from a different perspective is to discuss your problem. However, if you don't feel comfortable about this – don't worry. Imagine a friend coming to you for advice. Your friend is sharing each problem you have listed above. Listen to the problem and you will be able to see things differently. Analyse each problem on the list and look at the positive aspects they have brought into your life. For example: if you are worrying about money, think about how you can make some money. Does your home need a de-clutter? Could you make some money from selling unwanted items in your home? This turns the need for money problems into a reason to have a de-clutter (which is good for the mind – we feel better when our house is neat and tidy).

Selling the unwanted items may lead you to a new way of bringing a source of income. This is how I was inspired to start my eBay business. We were low on money and needed to raise the money to pay for a house move. I was inspired to sell some items on eBay and the rest is history!

EXERCISE #6

Make a list of five habits or people who are affecting your life in a negative way:

1 _____
2 _____
3 _____
4 _____
5 _____

Now you've established five things you need to pack in - it's time to set your goals how you will do this.

If you are smoking or drinking too much set a goal to reduce your intake.

Looking at how much money you are spending on your bad habit is a good way to motivate you. Work out how much you are spending a week then multiply it by 52. You will be amazed how much money you are spending on something that is having a negative effect on your life. Think about what else you could spend that money on – something that could you make you happy and bring you pleasure.

....
....
....

....
....
....
....
....
....

EXERCISE #7

Make a list of five people who bring joy to your life. These people need to be spirit lifters. These are people who you love spending time with and the time flies because you are having so much fun! Write their names down below and next to each name write the date of your next meet-up. If you haven't got a meet-up arranged, it's time to get in touch and arrange it. Spend time with people who bring you joy! If you haven't got five people to list, then get yourself out there and make friends.

_____   _____

_____   _____

_____   _____

_____   _____

_____   _____

....
....
....

EXERCISE #8

Take a few moments to reflect on the importance of personal responsibility in your life. Consider how it can positively impact your relationships, achievements and personal growth.

Write down three specific areas of your life where you would like to exercise more personal responsibility (e.g. health, finances, relationships).

....
....
....
....
....
....
....
....
....
....
....
....
....
....
....
....

EXERCISE #9

A good daily routine is to make a list of goals, chores etc. that you want to complete each day. Then go through the list and number them in the order they can realistically be completed. For instance, if one of the chores is food shopping and another is picking up a child from school. I would try to put food shopping before the school run as shopping is easier without a child in tow (and probably cheaper!)

Can you delegate any jobs on your list?

If you are finding, you are in a constant rush maybe you need to consider getting up earlier and trying a healthy pace.

....
....
....
....
....
....
....
....
....
....
....
....
....
....
....

EXERCISE #10

Make a list of 10 comedies, comedians, films etc. that make you laugh and lift your spirits. My partner's favourite film is ***Airplane*** and I must have seen it hundreds of times, but it still makes my partner laugh, which in turns make me laugh!

1 _____
2 _____
3 _____
4 _____
5 _____
6 _____
7 _____
8 _____
9 _____
10 _____

EXERCISE #11

Consider some recent setbacks you have experienced. What lessons have you learnt? Don't focus on the negatives and focus on the positives of the experience. Consider it a lesson learned and move on.

....
....
....
....
....

EXERCISE #12

Would you like to learn a new skill?

Well, what are you waiting for? Look on YouTube and find somebody to teach you. Start your research on the internet and see where it leads you.

Write down five skills or hobbies you would like to indulge in:

1 _____
2 _____
3 _____
4 _____
5 _____

Use this section to make notes of YouTube Channels you find:

....
....
....
....
....
....
....
....
....
....
....

EXERCISE #13
It's time to start looking at your life. What do you want out of our life? Are you putting others wants ahead of yours? Remember, needs and wants are different.

EXERCISE #14

Take a few moments to reflect on the aspects of your life that you appreciate and feel grateful for. Consider relationships, experiences, accomplishments and personal qualities.

Write down three things you are grateful for in your life right now.

1 _____

2 _____

3 _____

EXERCISE #15

Limiting Belief Identification:

Reflect on any self-imposed limitations or beliefs that hold you back from reaching your full potential.

Write down three limiting beliefs that you would like to overcome.

1 _____
2 _____
3 _____

....
....
....
....
....
....
....
....

EXERCISE #16

Is there past hurt or a fear holding you back from achieving the life you want.

Identify what is holding you back and how you are going to move forward by listing at least five goals to overcome these past issues:

....
....
....

EXERCISE #17

Most of us are good at talking but listening isn't always our strong point!

Engage in a conversation with a friend, family member, or colleague. Practice reflective listening by giving your full attention to the speaker. Resist the urge to interrupt or interject with your own thoughts or opinions. Instead, focus on understanding the speaker's message and emotions.

After the conversation, summarise what you heard and ask clarifying questions to ensure your understanding.

....
....
....
....
....
....
....
....
....
....
....
....
....
....
....
....
....

EXERCISE #18

Repeat these five affirmations daily:

I believe in my abilities and trust in my capacity to overcome any challenge that comes my way.

I am deserving of success, happiness, fulfilment and I have the power to create the life I desire.

I am confident in my unique talents and strengths, plus I embrace them fully to make a positive impact in the world.

I trust my intuition and make choices that align with my authentic self, leading me towards a fulfilling and purposeful life.

I am resilient, capable and worthy of achieving my goals. I will persevere and never lose sight of my unlimited potential.

Create your own affirmations for daily repetition:

....
....
....
....
....
....
....
....
....

....
....
....
....

EXERCISE #19

Examine your expectations of others and assess whether they are realistic or excessively high.

Identify three instances where you may have set unreasonably high expectations on another's actions, behaviours or responses.

Write down these instances and reflect on why you may have placed such expectations on them:

....
....
....
....
....
....
....
....
....
....
....
....
....
....

Whenever you notice yourself setting high expectations on others, pause and reflect on whether they are realistic.

Remind yourself that everyone has their own limitations and may not always meet your expectations.

Practice acceptance and understanding, allowing room for others to be imperfect whilst respecting their boundaries.

EXERCISE #20

Find a quiet and comfortable space where you can reflect without interruptions. Take a few minutes to reflect on areas of your life where you feel the need for improvement or change.

Consider how expressing yourself more effectively can contribute to these areas.

Write down three specific aspects of your life that you would like to improve through self-expression.

....
....
....
....
....
....
....
....
....
....
....

....
....
....
....
....
....
....

EXERCISE #21

Are you bottling things up?

Do you need to talk to someone and share your feelings?

If you don't feel like you want to talk to someone then watch a sad film and release those tears.

Write about what is making you feel sad and list five goals how you are going to overcome this emotion.

....
....
....
....
....
....
....
....
....
....
....

EXERCISE #22

Choose a person in your life whom you would like to better understand and connect with.

Set aside dedicated time to engage in a conversation with this person.

Practice active listening, paying close attention to their words, tone and non-verbal cues.

Put yourself in their shoes, attempting to understand their emotions, motivations and challenges.

Write about this experience and what you now understand about this person:

EXERCISE #23

Identify any limiting beliefs or self-doubts that may hinder your sense of empowerment.
Write down one limiting belief you want to overcome.

Challenge this belief by finding evidence or examples that contradict it.

....
....
....
....
....
....
....
....
....

Replace the limiting belief with a more empowering and supportive belief.

....
....
....
....
....
....
....
....
....
....
....
....

EXERCISE #24

Reflect on your current situation and identify areas where you genuinely need support.

....
....
....
....
....
....

Write down three specific needs or challenges that you believe could benefit from seeking help.

....
....
....
....
....
....
....
....

EXERCISE #25

Write a list of things that make you feel anxious. You cannot start to deal with anxiety until you identify what is making you anxious.

....
....
....

....
....
....
....
....
....

EXERCISE #26

Talk to your Guardian Angel every day. Make it part of your daily ritual: 'Good Morning Guardian Angel'.
Develop your relationship with angels and consider investing in some angel cards.

EXERCISE #27

Mindful Observation:
Begin each day with an intention to observe opportunities for acts of kindness.
Throughout the day, be mindful of the people around you and the situations that you encounter.
Notice moments where a small act of kindness can make a difference.

....
....
....
....
....
....
....

EXERCISE #28

Genuine Compliments:

Look for opportunities to offer sincere compliments to others.

Pay attention to their appearance, skills, or qualities that you genuinely admire.

Offer a kind word or compliment to at least three different people during the day.

EXERCISE #29

Random Acts of Kindness:

Perform at least one random act of kindness each day.

It could be as simple as holding the door for someone, offering a smile to a stranger, or helping someone with a small task.

Be creative and think of ways to brighten someone's day.

....
....
....
....
....
....
....
....
....
....

EXERCISE #30
Take a moment to reflect on past conflicts or disagreements you have experienced:

....
....
....
....
....
....
....
....
....
....

Consider how these conflicts affected your relationships and overall well-being.

Identify any patterns or behaviours that contributed to escalating the conflicts.

....

....

....

....

....

....

....

....

Cultivate an open-minded approach to disagreements. Remind yourself that different perspectives can lead to growth and new insights.

Acknowledge that you do not have to change your opinion but can still respect the other persons' viewpoint.

EXERCISE #31

Engage in critical thinking exercises or puzzles that challenge your ability to analyse information.

Solve riddles, logic puzzles, or brainteasers that require careful analysis and deduction.

Practice evaluating arguments, identifying logical fallacies and separating facts from opinions.

EXERCISE #32

Write down an area of your life which you feel you need to work on. Perhaps you had a skill that you stopped developing due to a setback.

EXERCISE #33

Identify areas in your life where you need to establish or reinforce boundaries. Reflect on situations or relationships that drain your energy or compromise your well-being.

....
....
....
....
....
....
....
....
....

Clearly define your boundaries and communicate them assertively and respectfully to others.

Practice saying "No" when necessary and prioritise self-care without guilt.

EXERCISE #34

Find time to meditate and sit in the silence. Focus on your breathing and live in the power of now. Find at least 5 – 10 minutes a day to let your mind and body be at peace.

Write down your feelings or visions you experienced during your meditation.

....
....
....
....
....
....

EXERCISE #35

SMILE

Go out and be mindful of how you present yourself to others. Smile at people and see how many people smile back. Write about your feelings and if this exercise has helped develop any new friendships:

....
....
....
....
....
....
....
....
....
....
....
....
....
....
....
....
....
....
....
....

EXERCISE #36

Inspired by the principle of Sing and Dance. At the end of this book, you will see my tracklist provided. I have chosen a relevant song for each principle, and I hope you take time to listen to each song and listen to the words. Write a list of ten songs that lift your spirit and instantly push your worries to one side:

1 _____
2 _____
3 _____
4 _____
5 _____
6 _____
7 _____
8 _____
9 _____
10 _____

EXERCISE #37

Write a list of five topics you would like to know more about? Is there a historic event that interests you? Would you like to research your family tree?

1 _____
2 _____
3 _____
4 _____

5 _____

Write down You Tube Videos and/ or books you have found to help you with your research:

....
....
....
....
....
....
....
....
....
....
....
....

EXERCISE #38

It's time to pamper yourself.

Book a date with yourself and do something that brings you pleasure. Write a list of five things you are going to do to pamper yourself. It could be a night in with a good film, a nice hot relaxing bubble bath, or a pamper night.

1 _____
2 _____

3 _____
4 _____
5 _____

Write down your ideal date with yourself and book it in!

....
....
....
....
....
....
....
....
....
....
....

These pages are for any additional notes you would like to make:

Printed in Great Britain
by Amazon